A Season with Marianne

The Last Surrealist

A Season with Marianne

The Last Surrealist

Alain Segura

Translated from the French by
Anna O'Meara and Sarah Lynne Roberts

COMMON NOTIONS
Philadelphia, PA
Brooklyn, NY
commonnotions.org

A Season with Marianne: The Last Surrealist

Translated from the French by Anna O'Meara and Sarah Lynne Roberts

Une saison avec Marianne, La dernière surréaliste aux Éditions PLEIN CHANT (Les Amis de PLEIN CHANT). Original French edition printed by Alket Editions in January 2022.

ISBN: 978-1-945335-15-0 | eBook ISBN: 978-1-945335-38-9
Library of Congress Number: 2024946884

10 9 8 7 6 5 4 3 2 1

Common Notions
c/o Interference Archive
314 7th St.
Brooklyn, NY 11215

Common Notions
c/o Making Worlds Bookstore
210 S. 45th St.
Philadelphia, PA 19104

www.commonnotions.org
info@commonnotions.org

Discounted bulk quantities of our books are available for organizing, educational, or fundraising purposes. Please contact Common Notions at the address above for more information.

Cover design by Josh MacPhee

Layout design and typesetting by Sydney Rainer / Suba Murugan

CONTENTS

NOTES ON THE TRANSLATION

When the translators first considered the following text, it was clear that style and contextual specificity were highly important to the author, Alain Segura, and his commitment to language and poeticism should inform our translation decisions.

We decided to consider methodologies used by the Situationist International, in particular those Guy Debord discusses in his collected letters, which reveal an intensive commitment to assisting translators in understanding his writing, clarifying meaning, and deep investment in etymology and double meanings. Words have histories and memories associated with them that are intangible and open. Following Debord's own methodology, the translators decided to engage Segura significantly in the process of choosing words and elaborating on the meaning of particular phrases. The translation of this text has the gift of the author's astute and poetic involvement.

The following deeply personal and literary account intends to recall a past through words; one defined by momentary interactions with the world that are now ineffable. Misty and soaked in spotted light, the text curves and winds, indicating a world in motion. Indeed, Situationists envisioned a world in flux with labyrinthine paths through life defined by "passages through brief moments in time." However, this text does not have the pacing of a labyrinth. It is not arduous, deliberate, entrapped, or ominous. Neither does it have the rapid sense of flight through an ever-changing world as one would find in Lautréamont's *Maldoror.*

The "curves" of the text, as Segura calls them, flow more like a stream. This dreamlike atmosphere similarly imbues the recollections of Marcel Proust. The blending of the real and the dream in the writings of Gérard de Nerval also greatly influenced the author. This text should not be labeled as a memoir or an account. It is neither a compilation of the entirety of a subject or an author's life, nor is it the result of a police interrogation. It fits, instead, the genre of the reverie. And what better style to commemorate Marianne Ivsic, the last Surrealist?

As for how the text relates to Ivsic, she has been a shadowy figure in the past, and she is not unearthed here either. There will be no exhumation, and this is based on her own wishes. Surrealist art sometimes dabbles, sometimes falls profoundly into the uncanny, the ephemeral, the unknown. Marianne, who requested a life in the shadows, shows how she admires these traits in her own artwork and in her own everyday life. Instead of tracing the facts of her life, this book provides a more intimate yet realistic impression: meetings with a friend. It makes us wonder what it would be like to learn the facts and details about the lives of each of our friends, who are all fleeting and mysterious in their own ways, and yet, they define who we are and our lives far more than a detailed biography of this-or-that historical figure might.

Segura, when asked for some words about where he might find more on Marianne, responded, "Could [these words be found] in a Buddhist monastery eight miles high, or in a Zen temple floating among lotus blossoms?" Perhaps both the horror and beauty of grief resonates in what is left unknown, and to a significant degree, unknowable even to the nosiest historians. We see this lack of accessibility as more of a Mount Kailash than a temple: there is something that exists, that is real, that is large and filled with evidence, but it is completely inaccessible to mortals. It floats in our minds like the heavenly abode ascribed to Shiva: mysterious, dangerous, beautiful, and filled with knowledge that we cannot attain.

ANNA O'MEARA *with* SARAH LYNNE ROBERTS

EXPLODING-FIXED[1]

At the end of June 2020, I received a request from two Serbian anarchists, Relja Knežević and Aleksa Golijanin, that brought back mostly buried memories from turbulent times. They decided to translate "Knights," which was an abbreviated title for one of my few publications, "Off They Go, the Knights on Their Quest" ["*Or s'en vont, les chevaliers questant*"]. After responding to their first message, I found myself inundated with questions about my friend Marianne, one of the main characters in my story.

Marianne signed one of the most beautiful pamphlets of May 1968 as "A Yugoslavian friend who knows things." She interested the two anarchists greatly because they'd discovered she knew members of the Situationist International. My text brought new insights to this subject, giving information about Marianne and her friendship with Guy Debord.

At first, I was uncertain whether I should answer them or stay quiet. Marianne liked to be secretive and nicknamed herself "Anonymous from the 20th Century." In her desire

1 "*Explosante fixe*," the original title for this chapter, references André Breton's *L'amour fou* (1937): "Convulsive beauty will be erotic-veiled, exploding-fixed, magical-circumstantial, or it will not be at all." André Breton, "L'Amour fou," *Oeuvres complètes* (Paris: Gallimard, 1992), 687.

to remain in the shadows, there was an enchanting playfulness and a tinge of vanity. In the end, we were able to shed a little light on her.

Outside of my text and Marianne's leaflet, my two correspondents knew little about the Situationist period. I provided them with contacts who gave them some photos of paintings that Marianne had gifted her friends. I assured them that really her only role in May '68 was writing her famous pamphlet, then distributing it in the streets, carrying a stack of copies in her arms.

I did a little research to unveil photos that illustrated where Marianne lived. Due to a love story, she found herself in an atelier in Ménilmontant in East Paris, where the Enragés and Situationists were active for a time. She captured attention when she brutally attacked a workerist who criticized a statue of Charles Fourier that was being built nearby. This was enough for Guy Debord—amazed by a fury that reminded him of André Breton and Antonin Artaud—to name Marianne "the last Surrealist."

Her friendship with Benjamin Péret spoke for itself.

The messages from Serbia kept coming and I answered them whenever I could. It got to the point that I had to stop collecting the messages. This challenged my commitment to staying silent.

In alchemy, as well as poetry, there is a black light. I tried to spread this, sure that only a black light has the explosive power of revelation. It produces successive but spaced flashes that the eye can only capture at the moment they escape, their disappearance assured.

Nothing comes before or after. Even less than nothing through this lens.

OPERATION MARIANNE

The initial contact from Serbia had some trouble reaching me. At first, a mutual contact refused to send me the message because of some trivial interpersonal conflict that found us at odds.

The story could have just stopped there or at least suffered a regrettable setback. As soon as I received his message, I expressed to my correspondent that I was pleasantly surprised by his responsiveness. This seemed like a good sign for future collaboration.

We aimed to better understand the trajectory of Marianne Ivsic, who had been Marianne Nikolic in 1944 when she took up arms to stand alongside the Yugoslav Partisans.[1] I needed to provide information about the period when Marianne settled in Paris around 1953. I'd known Marianne for a long time, since the fall of 1967. I had firsthand information thanks to our interviews, which occurred almost daily.

I dug up important original documents from my archives, some of which I had only a single copy. I set myself one initial

1 An antifascist resistance movement in occupied Yugoslavia during World War II.

objective: to collect photos that might reveal where Marianne had lived and the streets she frequented.

The Serbian correspondents were a historian and a translator. We spoke English in order to understand each other. Together, we advanced on two fronts: Yugoslavia and Paris. In large part, our research would be complete if we could successfully illuminate each location and bring them together. However, for the time being, the initial investigations were just beginning in each country.

A true wind of the steppe blew through the project. A furious maelstrom carried me away, shaking the very keyboard of my computer. The biggest challenge was Marianne herself, who had never ceased deliberately obscuring her trajectory, erasing every trace, and leaving next to nothing behind. There were some photos of her with the Surrealists and a few paintings that she'd given to friends. That's all that could be pieced together. In Paris, my friend Jean-Paul Coillot, who sculpted Charles Fourier, was someone Marianne really loved and admired. He could have spoken about her, but he adopted an extreme position: silence at all costs. We couldn't expect any revelations or reflections from him.

Should this also be my stance? I was uncertain. I couldn't decide whether I should speak or stay quiet. It had to be both. I'm not sure what led to my decision. Maybe I wanted to break a silence that Marianne didn't deserve but rather chose with a certain humor. (In other words, very seriously.) Yet, it was precisely her freedom that gave me mine. When I talk about her, I don't judge her decision or her desire to be silent. I was only putting myself in jeopardy. I couldn't imagine myself refusing to engage. I also somewhat admired the attempt by my Serbian friends to shed light with so few resources. Helping them seemed worthwhile. Marianne received little attention during her lifetime. I never thought of paying her a tribute, which she never would have wanted, with good reason. Yet it seemed right to bring her back to life as I'd known her, as much as she liked to hide, as much as she enjoyed "mystifying the world," to use an expression she liked.

In this state of mind, I entered a minefield, not set by an opposition but by the besieged herself: Marianne. Marianne, despite herself. "Ugh! Friends," she'd often say, "you can't count on them."

We never fought with her, and it was clear that we were rarely on her side. The first responses started flooding in and we took on water from all sides. But this position was firmly our own. And no one else has ever dredged this up.

I must say, as much in Serbia as in Paris, we managed to get closer to Alice Becker-Ho, René Viénet, and two of Marianne's Surrealist friends.

One afternoon, I found myself in a bookstore near the rue de Sèvres waiting to meet with René Viénet. Donald from New York, like René, had kind words for "Knights," the initial text where I spoke about Marianne. And how about

Alice, who searched her personal archives to find four photos of Marianne and Guy together in front of a house in Vosges where they stayed in August of '68? This unexpected evidence was something that my Serbian correspondents had heard about and relentlessly tracked for months.

Partly because of our efforts, a movement was coming back to life. One day, I told my Serbian friends with a smile that we could rebuild the Situationist International (SI), this time with an important section in the Balkans, a strong representation for parts of the world that the Situationists had never dreamed of—even at the height of the movement. Why is Marianne's memory important? Why revive the past of the Yugoslav Partisans and the Surrealists? For me, I often think about my father, who fought with the Spanish anarchists beginning in July 1936.

The worst thing would be acting as though none of this ever happened. So many people who fought fascism looked for help that they rarely found. Reconsidering them feels a bit like accompanying them up the mountain, helping them scale its slope, or handing them their rifle after they've lost it. It's important to create silence around them—even just for a moment—to stifle the incessant jabbering from the rest of the world.

Marianne lived in the building on the right, on the second floor. The cinema was opened after her departure for rue Charlot in the early 1970s.

This address, 42 rue Galande, was probably a sign for her: André Breton lived at 42 rue Fontaine.

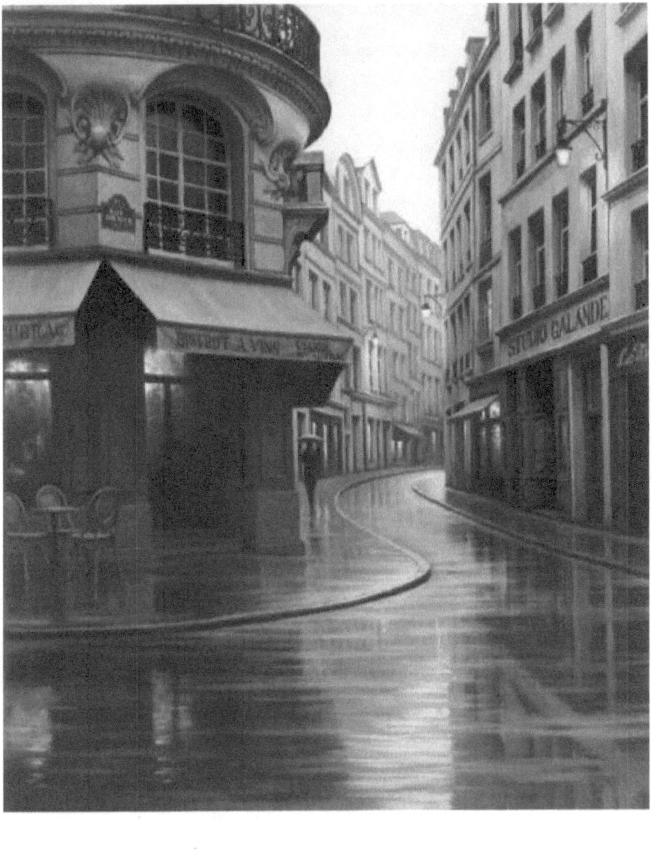
STUDIO GALANDE

When the renovators' hammers threatened the stone, Marianne, as a true adept and poet of the place, hurried to stop them.

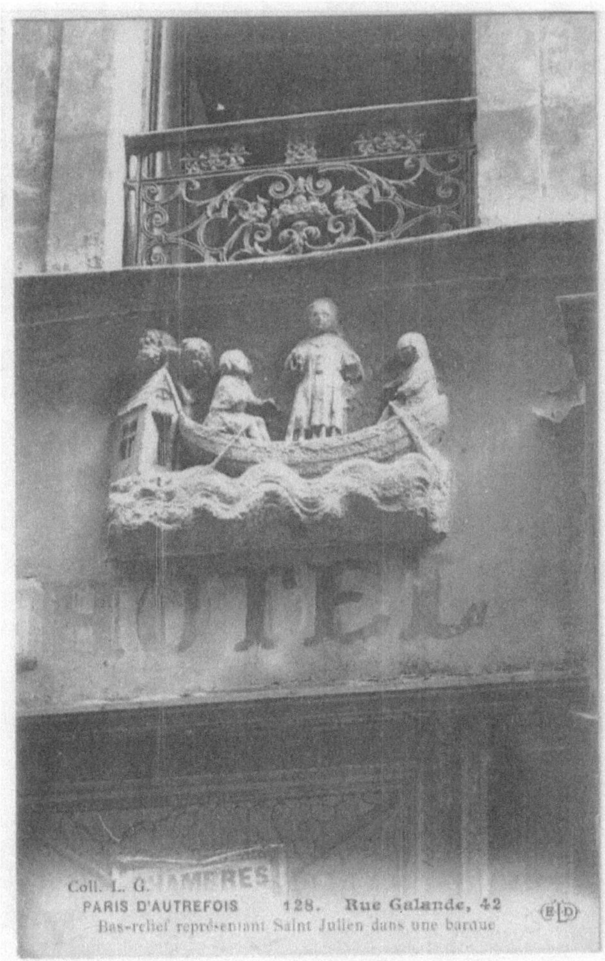
Coll. L. G.
PARIS D'AUTREFOIS 128. Rue Galande, 42
Bas-relief représentant Saint Julien dans une barque

OFF THEY GO, THE KNIGHTS ON THEIR QUEST[1]

To Roger Langlais

"Shining chain mail, glistening helmets, lances and shields, and gold and azure and silver." Like Perceval, I was dazzled. They moved through a network of alleys as though they'd known them forever. They liked cafés whose signs called with popular insurrection; they set the scenes of stories and made mysterious remarks. Seekers of the Castle Dangerous,[2] devotees of the High Science, they called themselves "Situationists."

In 1966, I was in tenth grade at Jean-Baptiste Say High School. Students my age in another class published a small zine with an anarchist tendency—a few poorly bound pages with splotches of ink that talked about the anniversary of the Hungarian Uprising and the Spanish War, if I remember right. I was vaguely aware of the history of the latter country, partly because my father had fled from there, but also partly

1 Alain Segura, "Or s'en vont, les chevaliers questant," *À contretemps* 40 (May 2011): 4–11.

2 The last of Sir Walter Scott's *Waverly* series of novels.

because I had a great teacher, who had his students translate the poetry of García Lorca.

I soon found myself invited to meetings with this anarchist group whose activity, even their existence, depended on a short young man with long hair and a black beard who signed nearly every article "René Riesel."

His dedication, along with his lively intelligence, earned him the goodwill of the teachers, whom he sometimes embarrassed. For example, one day in the auditorium, he began to belt out, "There was a little ship" ["*Il était un petit navire*"][3] to the great distress of an admiral who came to promote a film advertising the career benefits of the Navy. The lights came back on to show dismayed faces while the tune, now taken up in chorus, made the stands sway.

Smitten with radicalism, always on the lookout for new movements and trends, he peddled the zine at recess and went to Wednesday night meetings of the Liaison Committee of Young Anarchists ["*Comité de liaison des jeunes anarchistes*"].

This is how he heard about the famous "Strasbourg scandal." A small pamphlet had been published at the university's expense which said, in vivid language on a beautiful blue cover, *On the Poverty of Student Life* ["*La Misère en milieu étudiant*"]. The first time I read it, I didn't understand it. But there was a

3 A children's song about a young sailor about to be eaten by other sailors who consider which sauce to use while cooking him.

breath of fresh air in its presentation, joy, and a gift of truth. What's more, the diatribe did not leave the criticisms hanging but rather connected it to stronger trends before rekindling them. The plot seemed imminent. One paragraph after another addressed rambling isolated demands, leaving the option to embrace the global theory—a small flaw that the workers' councils would hasten to overcome.

Apart from the wonderful writing, the pamphlet proposed a universal remedy for the world. Rumors and chatter around its authors made it seem as though it were written by a mysterious brotherhood that was omniscient, invisible, and decidedly closed: the Situationist International.

I wanted to know more about them, and also to get their journal. Someone disclosed the address of a distributor to me, with the name of a metro station in a neighborhood I'd never been to before. As soon as I arrived, I was welcomed by a soft and muffled light, speckled by tall autumn trees that I have never seen again. The intersection opened on one side to Montagne Sainte-Geneviève, to the other, the river and the waterfront. I headed toward the rue des Boulangers, which rumbled with cobblestones back then.

I can picture that bookstore now, and the annex in the back, where I was guided. The back room was brighter than the shop because a garden light shone in through a half-open glass door. The journal, *Internationale Situationniste*, was organized chronologically on a large, polished wooden table.

The covers were metallic, shining like Christmas ornaments or sour candy wrappers after you scratch them with your nail. The glossy paper and ink had an intoxicating smell of almonds, which reminded me of the smell of the library in a small town where I'd once lived.

I still feel the clarity of sudden illumination from that day. Later, after I got to know the neighborhood, the Jardin des Plantes and the greenery of the rue Cuvier reminded me of my amazing discovery; of the leisurely tranquility and softness that dappled through that day.

Starting then, I tried to decode the journal without any preparation, never critical of the seductive dialectics that it proposed. At first glance, the photos in the journal, seemed to be unexplained by their captions. However, concepts were repeated in ways that played with multiple meanings that had a fascinating effect of highlighting the image, like a light that crackles all around then suddenly hits from behind.

The single word, destitution [*misère*], clearly lit up an ineffable feeling within. It brought me back to my childhood, my needs, my dismay when possessing a toy did not end but rather increased my emptiness.

"Commodity" is another word that had an emotional charge for me. In French, as "*marchandise*," it mixed something valuable with a sense of sweet delicacy. An entire theoretical structure was loaded with it, making it a key term I needed to consider profoundly.

"Revolt against the commodity," concerning setting Watts on fire. "The indulgences of the commodity," meaning what is granted freely, is always paid for somehow. In this game of mirroring, sometimes a sudden clarity arises. A moment of the world is seized.

The confident tone and well-composed sentences won me over, with a bit of an old-fashioned air borrowed from the great moralists. Their take on commodities was one of incredible disappointment but still held a sense of vanity and neglect.

I also loved the group photos, taken in harbors like Malmö during conferences. In a tucked-away room, around a long table, they seemed to be finalizing their words and testing some beers.

Sometimes, I went to meetings with René when they were held in locations provided by the exiled Spanish anarchists, the CNT. The critiques that came out of Strasbourg struck the anarchist movement, including the Anarchist Federation. *On the Poverty* mentioned its newspaper: "the incredible *Le Monde libertaire*, which was obviously written by students." Daniel Cohn-Bendit thought that was a bit harsh. An attack on such a great generation! And on its journalists! A section that was interested in Situationist ideas tried to give an objective account of their theories in a newspaper column. This section was rejected by the Anarchist Federation because it was labeled too "Marxist." It splintered into several new groups, a few of which merged to form the Anarchist International, which was basically founded on a platform of Situationist theories.

The Situationists were very prestigious. We were really honored when they granted us the favor of sending representatives. At first, both sides were somewhat timid as we found ourselves having drinks as a small group.

I took a chance and went to one of these meetings at a restaurant on the Place de la République. The two Parisian sections of the Anarchist International were represented. When I entered, I was struck by the restaurant's enormous, red back room which was completely empty apart from a table at the very rear where four young people were conversing. My comrades were already walking up to them, exchanging handshakes. All of my sixteen-year-old self-assurance and thoughtlessness were hardly enough to justify my presence. I was no longer simply curious, which wouldn't have been appropriate. These people inspired confidence in me. They had an aura of mystery, and the essence of their personalities merited our approach to them to the place where the drama was unfolding.

The only time I opened my mouth was to greet them. I have a vague memory of a question being asked—something about the SI's relationship to workers. This question seemed to me deadly out of place. However, René Viénet didn't bat an eye and treated it as very relevant. He even seemed slightly embarrassed to answer it, before mentioning a recent strike in Belgium.

We went out into the winter's night. In a windy corner of the square, René asked where we were headed and offered to accompany us to Les Halles. He pointed in its direction with one hand, tightening the collar of his shirt with the other. My friends politely turned him down. However, I followed him for a while, into the depths of a dark alley where old Paris seemed to find its end.

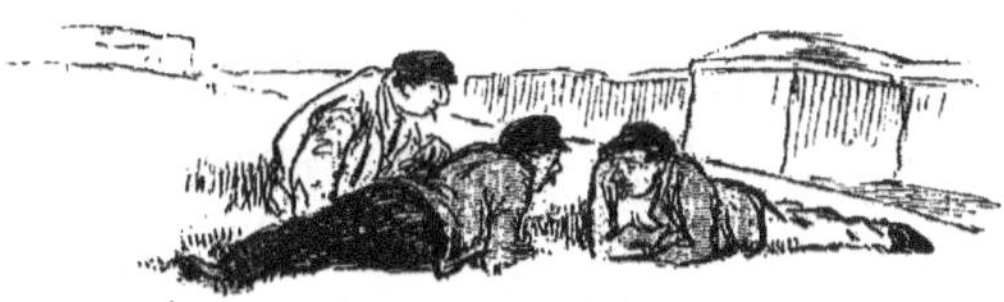

My anarchist friends picked a café in Les Halles for our meetings, which the Surrealists had often frequented, a heavy-handed attempt at a tribute. One evening, René Viénet showed up, our little troop followed his ample stride through the neighborhood to his place, where we'd been invited.

I remember a short trip in a single-file line, at nightfall, down sidewalks cluttered with crates. We stopped in front of an oak entrance to a robust square building with cut stone walls; between the walls and the roof were little windows that looked like a dollhouse.

At the bottom landing of a staircase, a row of steep, sonorous steps followed. Our host asked us to avoid making creaking sounds, adding with a smile that we were walking above his landlord's head.

We emerged into a loft, within an attic that had been converted into an atelier. Light filtered in from unknown places, leaving the unusual furniture partially illuminated. The edges of the attic were so warped that the floor touched the bottom of the mansard windows.

Two Situationists were there awaiting us: Donald Nicholson-Smith, whom I'd met with René Viénet at the Place de la République, and of course, Guy Debord.

Just saying his name sent a shiver, a thrill of mystery through us. He had a legendary intransigence, pulling as far from his enemies as closely toward his friends. We thought he had all the knowledge; that he was the embodiment of virtuosity. His contempt for all publicity made those who had the honor of knowing him flattered by the rare privilege.

In the only photo I'd seen of him, the smoke from his cigarette blurred his features. That night, he looked like a typical 1950s Left Bank bohemian, dressed in a sweater and corduroy pants. He had an alert, sharp glare behind thin-rimmed glasses, with a restrained hint of a scrutinizing and mischievous smile. His features were under the fringe of a short monkish hairstyle, except for a tonsure. His persistent smile veiled inner tension, but also revealed his grace and politeness as he welcomed us, each of the few times that I got to meet him. His words had a slow vibration and almost moralizing tenor, emanating a powerful intensity. Most of us sat on the floor, cross-legged, in his favorite position. I rested my shoulder against one of the small windows, at an angle so vertiginous that when I dared look to down, I felt as though I were flying above the street.

Guy Debord was not a conspirator or an unyielding dictator that some take pleasure in mocking. Sometimes this derision is out of bias, but sometimes there are people disappointed in the outcomes of their own ambitions who thus resort to dishonesty and bitter thoughts. Guy had a great influence and a disconcerting simplicity. When he came to a meeting, his powers of synthesis and rich contributions organically organized the discussion around him.

Another night, in a restaurant near the Gare de l'Est, I happened to sit across from him. I was holding a draft of a pamphlet that René Riesel requested I give the group at the meeting. He perked up with intrigue about the paper that I crumpled right in front of him after showing it to only my closest neighbors. He smiled and asked me to give it to him. On a simple sheet of paper, René had written a mock-up for the brochure's cover, which he intended to send to small groups who professed allegiance to a possible revolution: "You want to make a revolution . . . you need a global theory!" He lit up with a wide smile that seemed to question me. The idea only came from René, and I wanted to clarify that at all costs, I stammered: "It was René's idea . . . René's . . ." But the pamphlet was already being passed around everywhere; Guy was amused by the laughter that it inevitably elicited.

That night, he was wearing a very nice dark chevron sweater that he must have gotten at a conference abroad, maybe on the Baltic coast. One of our friends wore a matching sweater under her raincoat. We laughed at the coincidence. She bought it at a shop around Place des Ternes. Guy got his at Place Monge.

It's hard to imagine Guy walking through a market on a Sunday. But this unexpected deviation revealed a little bit about him, and it certainly moved me.

Mustapha Khayati was supposed to attend, to tell us a little about the recent events in Strasbourg. At that time, we were unaware of his primary role in writing the pamphlet, even though a press photo showed him with the students who were elected for their student government. The caption underscored the legend, "The mysterious MK of the Situationist International." He was so mysterious that he didn't show up, because he was detained at a dinner with some Arabic friends. Guy joked a little about this brotherly and ethnic meal before asking René Viénet to begin the presentation. René Viénet spoke with his usual liveliness. Guy stopped him right as he started: "No, René, that's not what happened. Start again, from the beginning, so that our friends understand." Guy sounded like a professor correcting a student who had started a presentation with the conclusion. We looked at him, incredulous, then paid even more attention given the weight of his interruption.

I've got to say this attitude became more pronounced over time, and admittedly it was often at our expense. In a discussion, he would move slowly, according to a succession of hard facts. Then, he'd suddenly bring in a connection, emphasized by an example from a book or film that everyone would agree with. He interrupted again to say that Mustapha should have never let himself be photographed with students that he did not represent. "That was his only mistake," said Guy.

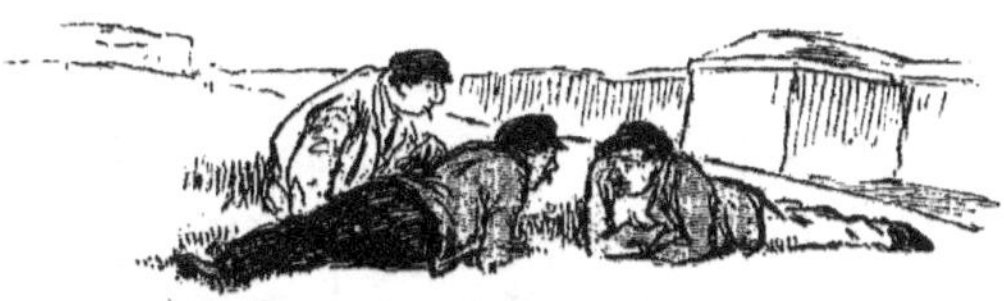

When I visited him later at his place on rue Saint-Jacques, I felt again what captivated me at the intersection of rue Monge and rue des Boulangers—that same soft and speckled light. I felt like I could almost taste the autumn through the tall trees. Time stood still there, like tension easing as a story unfolds. "Reinforcements!" called out Guy Debord as he opened the door for me.

That day, we were coming up with a response to a pathetic knock-off of a great pamphlet commissioned by the Makhno group in Rennes. One of our friends distinguished himself by finding the choicest phrases. But our group started believing that exclusion could make us more revolutionary. Which compelled the same friend, for reasons unknown, to pitch a program that had been met with strong support from the SI—to untangle anarchism from its many vestiges; just as the Situationists had detached themselves from various types of Marxism, past and present.

We showed up to back a dismissal, drafting a long memo for the Situationists, which I was tasked with mailing. Then we waited for a brief time. Almost immediately, a response arrived in a light envelope. Just a few simple and disengaged lines that differed from our extensive profession of faith made their disavowal apparent. We could have handled a step-by-step refutation, leading the Situationists to make high-level arguments. But these simple words revealed their disheartening judgment: our beautiful letter was contrived [*cousue de fil blanc*]. The next night, we were supposed to meet the Situationists for an exhibit of their comic strips. A terse postscript canceled the meeting, which they now found "unnecessary."

One little correction. But it made it clear that matters between us wouldn't move any further. Our faces, already contrite, dropped even further. We were kicked out of the party, from libations, from the ongoing procession of serious practice, and each of us was sent back devastated. Deprived of the support guaranteed by this important alliance, our group soon withered away.

Some stopped being interested in theories. Others would rediscover a simpler path, confident that the defeat of this group wouldn't stop them from other endeavors in the future.

A little later, in November 1967, Guy published his book, *The Society of the Spectacle* [*La Société du spectacle*].

The Strasbourg pamphlet summed up central Situationist ideas. The strength of this pamphlet was in its cutting critique. The seduction of its solutions positioned it among the greatest libels of the past few centuries because it took up their cause—heightened exasperation, promising the advent of a better time, ending in the rediscovery of an eschatology. Some remarkable figures endorsed it with sincerity and integrity, and no one doubted them. It had a confident tone compared to other rationales for the destitution [*misère*] from various groups of the time. The elegant overarching analysis provided the endeavor with a sense of undeniable authenticity.

Guy's effort was excessive and endearing. *The Society of the Spectacle* seemed to promise to remove the veil, even though I was never convinced by this book's moralizing tone and weighty declarations. However, I wasn't left indifferent as I considered the title in black letters and the dazzling white cover. I sensed a concern with holding the words, even just retaining their shadow, as though the world, now captured, must remain imprisoned in ink, never to escape from the page.

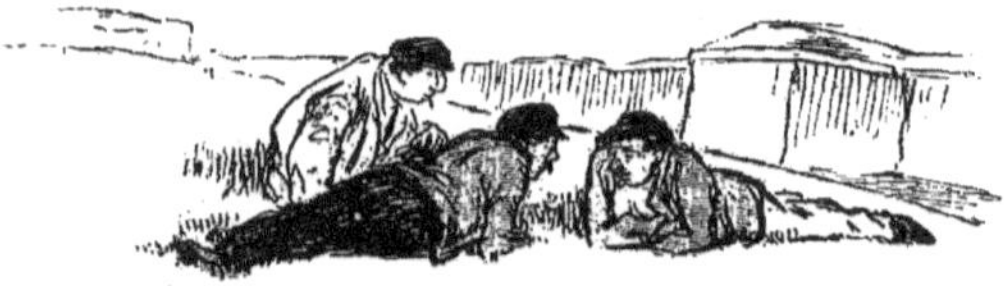

I kept visiting the local anarchist youth center. At the entrance, an old Spaniard ran a stall with books, brochures, manifestos, and announcements from the anarchist presses in exile. He was a worn-out, tired, short man. His entire retirement was spent at the top of a staircase that smelled of disinfectant.

Our meeting room looked like a high school study hall. A coal furnace hummed in the corner, and chairs were scattered around a few benches. It was kind of like a garret, which gave it a conspiratorial air. It was like those ateliers in old engravings where oppositional statements were written amid smoke, emanating from the smokers' pipes as much as the leaking chimney ducts. One night, a door opened at the back of the room. Heavy silhouettes glided through the swinging doors. We suddenly fell silent while men in dark suits passed through our ranks. They smiled shyly as though they were embarrassed to interrupt us, but also because our age reminded them of their past and confirmed the emergence of naive successors.

A photo in an issue of *Internationale Situationniste* displayed captured militants being taken to their execution. I often scrutinized their expressions. The only concern I saw was managing not to trip on their shackles and chains or the piles of frozen dirt in the furrows. The men who passed in front of me recalled that unfortunate procession.

One day I was sitting at a restaurant table cracking open an issue of *Internationale Situationniste*. A man approached me. He knew about the journal and was eager to talk about it. He was Spanish, and after we befriended one another, he confided that he was a member of a younger section of the CNT which began to contest previous certainties about exiles. I told him about my Spanish background and name. He looked at me, shocked: "Wow, that means I know your father. . . . He often comes to meetings." I was totally unaware of my father's membership to the anarcho-syndicalist union, and even more surprised that he'd remained active. In a flash, I attend a meeting of the outreach committee. Through the back door, left ajar, I see my father leaving.

Then, came the pressing memory of a voice from my first trip to Spain. I was thirteen. Darkness had fallen at the winemakers' cooperative, and a film was about to start. A hand brushes my shoulder, and I hear a man whisper, asking about my identity before telling me to relay a message to my father, along with a name I mustn't forget.

I saw my father, too, in that photograph of captured militants. Once, he told me a story about an ambush. He reached a village, retreating there, while still on the run from the enemy. The next day, he woke up first and looked outside. The enemy was near, just around the corner. My father barely had time to warn his companions.

In Paris, he found a best friend, a refugee like him who was from the same village. I went with them downtown to a small cinema one night. The room was packed. The audience shuddered as a montage of news footage from the Spanish Civil War played. The chatter was incessant, and then amid the noise arose a song from the Revolution, and the crowd immediately joined in chorus.

For the exiled, time is a stopped clock whose hands need to be set back before they can start again. It's an empty dial where time has collapsed. I felt this abyss one day in Barcelona in front of an immense building covered in gray dust. My father showed us: "These were the barracks where we left for the front." He smiled as he remembered the name because, he said, it had changed a long time ago; more than thirty years had gone by. But as soon as he spoke this name aloud, the car suddenly stopped.

Ongoing traffic closed in on us. An onslaught of menacing waves, screeching sirens, and glimmering rain gushing under the wheels of the tram. We were stuck in the past, like a haunting shipwreck that would soon be entirely submerged. . . .

Nothing has happened on this trip so far. There are no taxis but old carriages are able to make it through to the center of the city. There are few people on Paseo de Colón. But, at the entrance to the Ramblas (the main street in Barcelona), we were shocked: a revolution flashed right before our eyes. It was incredible. It was as though we were entering a different continent like none we had ever seen. The first image: armed workers with guns on their shoulders but dressed in civilian clothing. Almost half of the men on the Ramblas were armed. We didn't see any policemen or soldiers in uniform. . . . Only a few of these armed proletarians wore the new militia clothing, which were well-fitted mechanic's overalls in smart navy blue. They sat on benches talking, and walked around, one arm holding the strap of their rifle and the other around their partner's waist.

For the first time, I'd discovered a city in the hands of the working class. Almost all of the main buildings were occupied by workers and they flew red flags or the red and black anarchist banner on their façades. All of their walls bore the hammer and sickle, along with acronyms of revolutionary parties. All of the churches had been ransacked and set on fire; now, teams of workers were demolishing them. Big posters in stores and cafés announced collectivization. Even the shoeshines were collectivized; they carried their gear in a red and black box.[4]

4 These quotations from George Orwell's *Homage to Catalonia* (1938) and Franz Borkenau's *The Spanish Cockpit* (1937) indicate memories of past rumblings from the street.

A van towed us, but the chain broke twice before the clamor of George Orwell's *Homage to Catalonia* and Franz Borkenau's *The Spanish Cockpit* faded behind us.

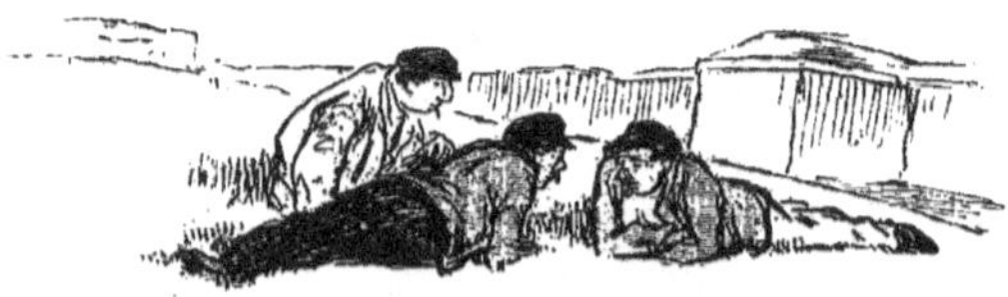

René decided to take his final graduation assessments [*le bac*] early, at the end of the 12th grade, and he planned to pass on the first try. In the fall of 1967, he showed me the Nanterre-La Folie campus. I had never seen anything more squalid and ultimately desolate. Aggressive and constraining urban planning spoke volumes about the contempt of the powerful for lumpen proletarian students. The destitution of the surrounding slums didn't seem quite as uncompromising, and, more importantly, it didn't seem as intentional.

I'm still frustrated by the flow of the pathways, which was based on new designs for movement through prisons. Large plastic palm trees shaded the neon lights of the cafeteria.

I knew Gérard Bigorgne—tall and gangly, he had bushy hair and a distinguished manner, he never became like the bohemians around him, and he never claimed to have a bohemian lifestyle.

I've forgotten all about his actions in Nanterre with René and the other Enragés except for the first pamphlets, that refused student status and spoke of its adaptation by modernist protesters.

One of these tracts took a comic strip out of an old newspaper showing a group of thugs chatting in a college pub about predictions for the future of the laws of the market, as though they were just checking boxes, a game they'd long played.

In this legendary tavern in Les Halles, I remembered how, in "The Crowned Radish" ["*Le Radis couronné*"] chapter of Théophile Gautier's novel *Le Capitaine Fracasse*, Jacquemin Lampourde sat alone at a table, in front of two glasses, waiting for a guest. I imagined this companion, but I instead called him "Lancelot Bigorgne," to fit the story better.

It was May 1968. A comrade from the Ménilmontant group had been working on a project for a while—it was taking shape in his atelier—an homage to the author of *Le Nouveau monde amoureux*, Charles Fourier. Gérard was posing for the Fourier statue. The sculptor was having trouble with the crease in his pants, and he still remembers how gracious this Enragé was. He had even helped transport a heavy bag of plaster to the site of the sculpture's construction.

The sculpture was met with a certain hostility from members of the Anarchist International "Knights," which was an abbreviated title for one of my few publications, "Come What May, The Knights will Quest" ["*Or s'en vont, les chevaliers questant"*]. The most disapproving was the same individual who'd asked René Viénet about the Situationists' relationship to workers.

Marianne spoke up. She launched into a vicious indictment, expressing her frustration to the Situationists.

I had met her shortly prior to May 1968. The friend who I was with had plans to meet her in a café on the Place de l'Odéon. Marianne was in her fifties. Slim, elegant, and armored with a long, black oilskin coat, her eyes hidden behind sunglasses. She was holding a cigarette case stocked with Gauloises. Her alert posture distinguished her from the few other people, most of whom were lounging on the balcony. I lingered briefly under the pretext that a conference on *autogestion* was starting shortly at the Sorbonne. Until then, I hadn't noticed her staring at me. Then, lightning struck:

"Who is lecturing?"

"The author of a book about anarchy."

"Every idiot is going on about '*autogestion*' these days without knowing what they're talking about."

I arranged to meet her again in a few days at a restaurant near the Louvre, which was also the set of the TV series *Belphégor*. Her long, dark silhouette against a red bench looked like the recurring vision of a ghost.

I soon came to understand that around her, nothing could be assumed. When I pulled up a chair to take a seat, she'd stare at me with commanding superiority to catch me off guard. She'd make it clear that this was not simply a friendly meeting.

During our meetings, I stood at a distance, looking at the glimmer of the exit from the well-orchestrated flashes of her fury. "Dammit, I am an intellectual! I admit it!" The expert thinkers, the truly repentant intellectuals who'd disguised themselves as workers, or as true workerists, also took their share of criticism. People usually tried to justify themselves to her.

I also noticed how often people felt the need to justify themselves. We always felt guilty because we could never live up to her expectations. I was confused but amazed by her brilliance, her way of shutting down ideas with citations from great minds. When anyone was deemed suspicious, they would hear the motto, "Poetry equals Love equals Freedom." She proclaimed this Surrealist credo, which few have cared to explain, all the time, in every possible way, at unexpected moments, but unfailingly. This was sometimes uncomfortable, especially as the situation did not always warrant this battle cry.

I remember how she hated the word "liberation," which was very fashionable at the time. "A slave word. Liberation will never be freedom." I'd recently found an alchemical engraving of a dog crawling with its belly in the dirt after breaking its chain. Yet, the collar, with the chain links hanging, was still around its neck. He was crawling like an escaped runaway. I tried to translate one of the Latin riddles on the engraving.

Marianne clarified in just a few words. "Marvel," she said, "can appear at the first street corner, but the world is stifled under the weight of conventions and the depressing vapidity of routine."

Insurgent, fiery, and rebellious, as soon as she felt that someone was beginning to talk about common assumptions, she'd consider her interlocutor coldly, look them in the eyes, and then set them ablaze: "Nonsense! Think with your head! All idiots have ideas. It's the thought that counts. And watch your words . . . if you use them improperly, they come back to avenge themselves."

I knew her through two addresses, both of which were marked with her seal. The first, on rue Galande, was medieval. It was located on steep ground. It was rumored that Dante had once lived there, which was suggested by documents from his time. Dante must have known a Paris with beautiful street signs swinging in the wind, dreamy walks through winding corridors, and tall houses with pointed roofs whose gables got lost in the mist.

The door opened to a dark corridor that led to a large, red-tiled room beneath a ceiling of brown-stained beams. There was a library in one corner and a long oak table with two benches in the other. Sitting there was like stopping at a roadhouse next to a crossroad in the passage of time. An elbow on the table brushed with renowned presences from the past.

Marianne lived frugally but hated poverty [*misère*]. She claimed that she gave herself the luxury of poverty because she was opposed to success at all costs. She'd leave that to the schemers or all those people who had nothing better to do. She favored a quote by Benjamin Péret: "Even a single hour of work a day is an hour too much." She saw no contradiction in her meticulous application to her part-time jobs. "Work is shit. But it gives me the freedom not to let it clutter my brain afterwards." After work, Marianne was at her friends' disposal. She listened to them and always seemed to find a core element in pieces by painters, sculptors, and writers that she strove to magnify—their mercury. But this mercury has a volatile nature. It wants to escape without being controlled. "Listen to it carefully. It's trying to talk to you, amidst your worries. And it has so much to say."

Discussing problems with her didn't mean finding resolutions. She'd derive the secret collusions between the words leading to a completely different discussion that would end with us bursting into incredible laughter.

Whenever the topic of beauty came up, her criticism was uncompromising. "Beauty annoys me. I don't give a damn about it." She often told a story about André Breton. He was coming out of a gallery, making a fuss, while saying, in an affected tone, "It's beautiful." Marianne mimed the scene, acting out and waving her arms with such dejection that she almost fell forward.

"Benjamin . . . adoration. . . . And André, there was always a little wave when I'd arrive at the café. . . ." Marianne talked about their long friendship a lot. It sometimes felt embarrassing to watch, as though she'd introduce herself by saying, "Hi, my name is Marianne, and I was friends with André Breton and Benjamin Péret."

I had become a regular at rue Galande, devoted to endless talks and readings. I saw Marianne's attitude change. She had a lively nuance as she expressed her thoughts. She would turn to thank my silent approval with a flutter of her eyelashes. There were five of us, sometimes four, often three. Marianne didn't like big groups; a select few benefitted from one-on-one meetings with her—and if possible, among themselves.

"Rue Galande is a fortress. That is why André was able to come here and take refuge during the Algerian War when he was in danger. He'd raise his forehead and put a finger to his lips, then get up, walking with big steps, slowly, as he tried to remember verses of the poems with so much inspiration and such a voice."

Draped in centuries-old cloth, rue Galande was never bathed in sharp or intense light. I would always climb the small stairs into the mist of another era, into the fine dust that covers a book falling apart at the spine.

The day after she had her outburst in the atelier, Marianne heard a knock at the door. It was René Viénet. He took a blank canvas from a package and covered it in a bluish-purple pigment. He stuck a toy car in the center, then doused it in gasoline and set it on fire. Afterward, patiently, he wrote in white calligraphy at the bottom of the canvas: "This will be the car of the workerist Hubert B if he continues to piss off those brave devils, the Enragés, who never asked him his opinion of Fourier."

He stuck the painting on the wall himself where it would hang until it got lost in a move. But it remains untouched in my memory, where I think of it fondly. Maybe one day, I will try to reproduce it to make it more than an ephemeral moment from another time.

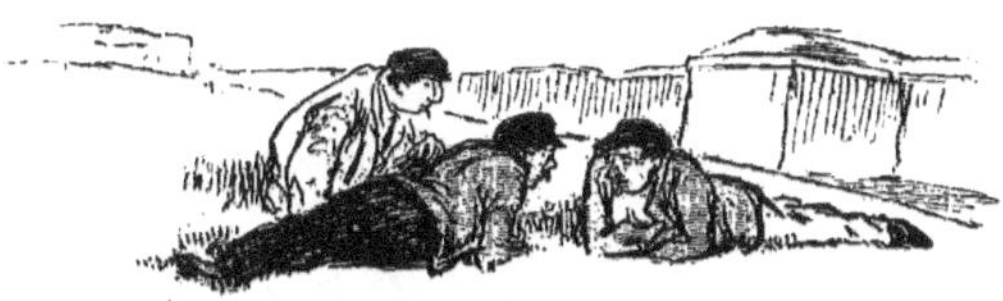

I never agreed, for a single moment, with the May '68 crowd. The movement of occupations asked society to stop and to sever ties with the world. But beneath their charts of demands, the barriers had not given way. They had only multiplied.

One day, in an auditorium, I was surprised by the clear, thunderous voice that tried to bring some succinctness and light to open debate. It was René Viénet attempting to intervene. He was worthy of the greatest revolutionary assemblies;

at first, he was met with applause that later devolved into common heckling.

At the front, on stage, I recognized all the faces from the Liaison Committee of Young Anarchists (CLJA) I used to see at Wednesday night meetings. Their chaotic display was so arrogant that they took pride in abusing the right to representation. Below the stage, factions stirred up in sedition, waiting to take over the place.

Slogans hung from the walls, but they felt redundant as soon as we had read them.

"Destroy power without seizing it," Marianne said, in one of the most beautiful leaflets from May '68. Guy Debord called her "the last Surrealist." He wondered if that was a reason to rejoice or complain.

To rejoice, of course. When the Surrealists, overwhelmed with absurdity, wrote on a sticker, "The Surrealists are at your service, students," Marianne replied indignantly, "Just the word 'service' already makes me want to vomit."

But also, to complain. When Guy said: "Benjamin and André waited in vain for this," seeking validation, Marianne grimaced with reluctance: "I'm not sure they would have jumped for joy."

Marianne wasn't fooled by the rioters who claimed to be spontaneous, nor by the pseudo-councilism of the occupation movement.

Marianne saw the stakes differently, as a unified desperation. She called for, without contradiction, a "revolution made by happy people." According to her, they were the only ones who wouldn't give in to the vertigo of power, something that freed slaves would always be fated to do.

"We can't blame the world for the barriers it puts up before us, as much as for the screens that hide its possibilities."

"Irrational and too subjective," Debord concluded. Marianne still bothered him with her compulsion to annotate his copy of *Le Monde* every afternoon: "Poor Guy, you are absolutely missing out on poetry."

However, a mutual respect, even a real friendship, soon brought them together, which can be seen in the copy of *The Society of the Spectacle* that Marianne later showed me: "To Marianne, whom I have always loved."

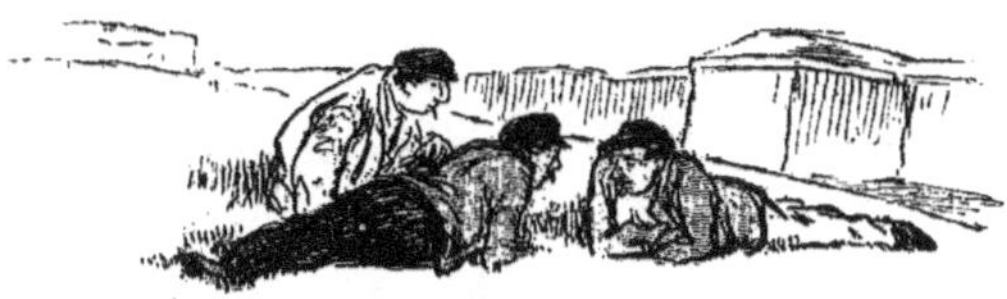

At the end of the summer of '68, I returned to Paris after a long stay in Collioure, in the foothills of the Pyrénées, where I saw a student who I knew from high school. His parents used to own an old hotel, but it had long since closed. It became a refuge for many exiles after the Spanish Civil War. The poet Antonio Machado blessed it with his presence before ending his life there.

The post-May '68 period brought together protesters from every region and country to Coullioure. These people were of unclear allegiances and, for the most part, entirely opportunistic. If their word is to be believed, they were the creators of the storm that was barely over: rivaling the fires, the explosions, and the barricades everywhere. The rioters on the beach were still searching for cobblestones beneath the sand.

However, there were also specific people who had a more reserved demeanor, almost secretive, not concerned with being seen or counting the cans of gasoline that they'd lit. The most ferocious ones hadn't waited for May's boat to drift away. One of them carried everything he owned in a small bag, that he'd sometimes empty of all its contents, reaching toward the bottom of the bag for a precious companion that wandered with him, always there for him in his solitude. I was very familiar with the cover, with its large black letters: a pocket edition of Comte de Lautréamont's *Les Chants de Maldoror.*

In a story, Axel would have been a page, or maybe a cobbler or woodcutter.[5] During his travels, he'd learned a thousand and one trades, all of which he did not consider to be drudgery.

---

5 Axel Bogousslavsky (1937–2023) was a guitarist and later, a great actor. Patricio Ullao Rubke worked in Germany as a dance professor. I met them both in Collioure around the same time. —Author's note.

He liked to remember their unique spirit, and in this regard, his knowledge was far from fragile.

Axel would play guitar with the movement and quick pacing of a Roma [*manouche*] in pursuit of a fleeting memory. I'd never heard such inflections in playing before, but he added them to each song he played. He had a great affinity for an old tune, a favorite that I always requested from him: "Ménilmontant."

Patricio was Chilean, born in Germany. He made his living working short seasonal gigs where he got to know old Spanish fishermen in exile. Methodical and aloof with an aristocratic air, he knew how to make every moment of the day feel like a party. A small group occupied the ruins of a castle on the hill with him. He'd make dinner for them from the leftovers that he'd charmed the vendors at Les Halles to give him, with a smile.[6]

I returned to rue Galande in the fall. A young man who wore a bright-green corduroy suit had become a regular. It was especially strange because he wore it every day. He was the sculptor of Charles Fourier, for whom Marianne offered her apartment as a studio. I spent one night with him on a café terrace. That night, two young women at the table next to us were staring. Jean-Paul Coillot began to get very annoyed,

6 At the Marchand in Les Halles, vendors sold leftovers from the surrounding restaurants.

particularly because, for a while, he seemed to be the object of their insistent looks. These two beautiful women, making no effort to hide it, were exchanging comments. Jean-Paul got up and walked over quickly. I watched him lean over their table then abruptly turn around, returning to his seat, while making a sweeping gesture, as if trying to shake off his irritation.

"Do you know them?" I asked.

"Not at all."

"Then why . . . ?"

"I don't know . . . I suppose, to them, I look just like a romantic lead from the movies."

I felt guilty for smiling. Jean-Paul moved on to another topic. But his beauty, if we must account for it, was that of an archangel, it could never be seen without fear. The awkward words of these two young women may simply have been describing this miracle with great and beautiful innocence.

His vivid resemblance to the profile and face of young Artaud, combined with the imagined portrait of Lautréamont by Félix Vallotton, was coupled with another beauty far more disturbing, the one within.

After leaving Marianne's place, we would take long, winding walks—*dérives*—prolonged by an intention to get lost at night. As morning met us with warm mists of dew filling empty streets, the revelations we searched for, day after day, seemed inevitable and imminent. We'd often pass out, exhausted, on benches, and phrases from a book found in some alley, chosen for its appealing title or cover, would emerge like echoes, responding to our conversations.

Soon enough, the Situationist International no longer existed. Guy Debord declared its dissolution when it had been replaced by a mere shell of itself, surviving out of vanity. Only to keep producing, year after year, a journal for its increasingly large audience, trusting in a name that was recognized everywhere.

Many years later, long after I lost any contact with former Situationists, I bought *Panegyric*, a short book by Guy Debord that had just been published. I read it that day. For the first time, Guy spoke about himself and his life's journey in detail, even if he still employed a distanced tone to avoid any undesired attention.

Suddenly, it hit me: I remembered the name of a street where he'd been seen a few weeks before. I took a short walk there that evening.

The rue du Cherche-Midi still bustled with the same old crowd. The street begins as a curve of elegant old mansions that blend above the wide arches of their entrances. They were just a few stories, with tall windows and dormers flooded with a view of the peaceful sky.

My steps searched the dusk. I changed my path, reading a signboard, when I found Alice and Guy in the middle of the street.

They walked toward me peacefully, leaning against each other. Alice matched Guy's uneasy and tired pace. They didn't see me pause, or my surprise, when I came across them. Guy talked with downcast eyes as Alice listened with an assuring smile. Without lingering, I crossed the street to admire a circular bas-relief portraying an astronomer, surrounded by instruments; he seemed to be working under the sage advice of a child. The compass in the old man's hands could have pointed to the very spot of a meeting, which I had been unaware of that very morning but whose urgency I had felt mounting throughout the day.

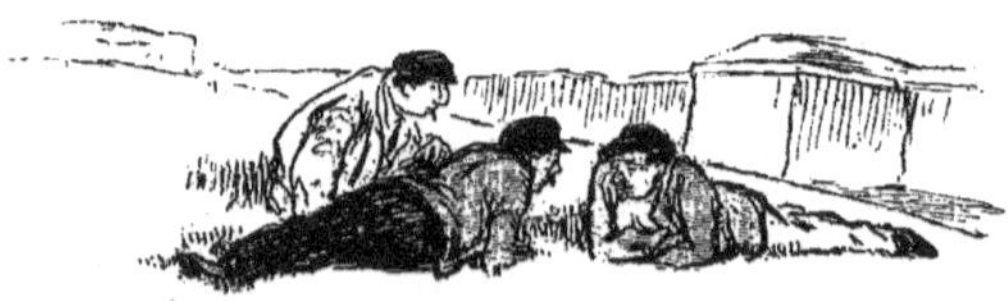

One Sunday near the Louvre, I ran into Jean-Paul, who gave me Marianne's new address in the Marais. She was somewhere on rue Charlot. I didn't have the exact address, but he gave a clear description of a porch leading to an atelier. Marianne's name was written on the door. I ventured there one magically fanciful night. The bus to the Hôtel de Ville station left me alone in the wind. I had a path in mind, through vertical lines of streets that led upward, crosscut by a series of horizontals that were supposed to bring me closer.

I had no idea how often I would end up making this trip, or how, on later trips, my course would drift around the angle of an old wall, bypassing it, and that the singular glow of a streetlamp would only make the surrounding darkness look darker. I was taken aback by the stifling weight of timelessness, which had not been shaken off in the centuries since. A half-open gate led to a door through a courtyard; upon it, "Marianne" was written in chalk. I knocked a few short times. Nobody answered.

I walked toward the intersection. A few storefronts were still open that night. A figure takes leave of a passerby, then turns to me and says, "That was a friend who I haven't seen for a long time and who has come from far away."

The entry for rue Charlot in the *Historical Dictionary of the Streets of Paris* [*Dictionnaire historique des rues de Paris*] is illustrated with two photographs. The first shows the intersection where I rediscovered Marianne. The second shows the entrance leading to her atelier. "An entrance under a vaulted ceiling first leads to a picturesque courtyard, which opens to a staircase to an old house at the back." I later found on an old postcard from a series entitled "*Paris d'autrefois*" ["Old Paris"] a shot, from the same angle, of the "doorway of a very old house, notable for its beamed ceiling." One small lamp lit the entrance where I stood beside a long trestle workbench cluttered with pens, pencils, quills, and brushes. A canvas on an easel screened the darkness that devoured the back of the studio.

But what really stood out, like the arched frames in an illuminated manuscript, was a corbel, held up by a fine framework of grooved wooden beams. The structure of the old house rose above this overhang. "I saw its marvel immediately," Marianne told me. "But I had to deal with tons of rubble. I started by axing it, then I finished with a knife."

A thin line of cobblestones led the old alley toward the back of the courtyard. The other side, under the beams, passed through the atelier. From what I could make out, this path was the most well-hidden. It was as though it was illuminated by nothing, but still somehow aglow.

I brought a manuscript. I didn't get to spend much time there that first night. I stood by Marianne as she thought about the title in black letters: "WARRIOR (in English), what a fantastic word. Where did you find this?" I wanted to explain, and I started to translate. She stopped me immediately. "Don't bother. Reading it tells me everything: *VARIE OR* [varied gold], he who changes gold."

Today, I go there with my camera. I frame the door of the atelier with the viewfinder, a door that Marianne no longer opens. I can't get the shot to focus on the little label that has long replaced the bright chalk letters. Maybe I'll get some photos inside later.

When the door opens, I decide against the idea. Two days prior, I learned that she had died. A gray fog floats in the space of the atelier. The shining sun floods the courtyard, but the glass roofs have become clouded in the daylight. What was there for my camera to capture? The spirit of the place had been extinguished. From that moment, I decided to leave. And to never come back.

A great springtime high wind blows a sharp and biting air this morning that once met Marianne at her doorstep. "Paris," she'd say, "is on the coast of the ocean."

With a final wave goodbye, I disappeared under the large porch. For one last moment, as I passed the roofs, I felt a pull, an invisible shiver. I hurried through the alleys of the Marais, then switched course in a *dérive*, which changed depending on the time, the light, signs that called to me, and the scent of the wind. I experienced every season, every twilight, every silent nightfall, when I went back there. I clutched the pages that I'd just read in the atelier, which now felt so much more precious.

My chair leans into the edges of darkness. Darkest night surrounds the atelier. By a small table—the only one with a light—Marianne sits up straight. The lamplight forms a halo around her profile. Her eyes move rapidly, taking vigilant glances.

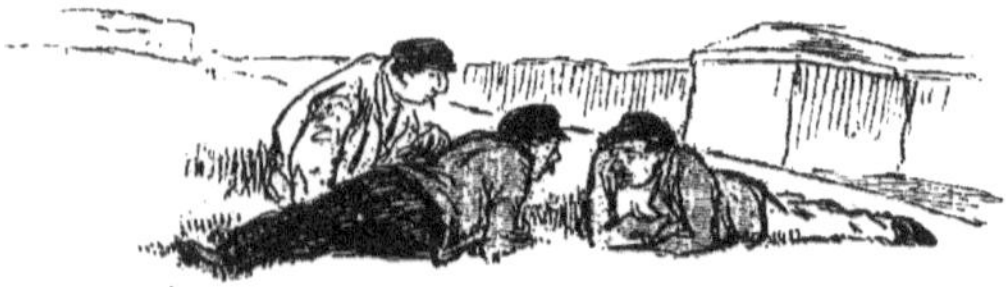

"It's incredible," lamented the book dealer, "It should have been recorded. . . ." I stopped in front of his book display—a pile from every revolution. At first, I thought he was talking to himself, but he noted that I was perusing a small brochure on Spain. "I was told everything about this and more once in a café. He knew a lot about it, the old man not from having read it, but because he was there. . . ." He then paused, savoring my surprise. I was intrigued, indeed, but mainly by the café's location. "Over there, toward Les Halles, between rue de Rivoli and the Quays." His hand gestured across the river, tracing a small islet that I knew very well—as well as the café under my own building.

For several months, my father had helped me restore a "musketeer's lodge," as I immediately referred to it, which smelled like freshly stained wood, and was accessed by open-air stairs.

The café was in a little enclave on the ground floor like a tavern from antiquity. He talked about the conversations with the regulars. One day, he talked about Spain with a used book dealer: "You should go meet him." He'd told me afterward, "because he knows a lot."

My book dealer now said the same thing years later. Maybe I should have talked to him and introduced myself. But he kept on shaking his head as though lost in a dream from a book that was impossible to recreate. He liked telling the customers who passed by, rummaging around, that he was the only one who knew about a book that they could never find.

I stepped back to convey my surprise. But I should've been surprising him. Rereading *Homage to Catalonia*, I was surprised to find that, in the revolutionary city, George Orwell joined the militia as they were preparing to leave for the front. They were in former cavalry barracks that had been taken a few weeks earlier and victoriously renamed the "Lenin Barracks."

This was the same name that my father had mentioned in front of the old building in Barcelona.

TWENTY YEARS AFTER

For Relja and Aleksa

What would happen if I retraced my steps through the square at the Hôtel de Ville to Marianne's workshop on rue Charlot? When I think of that square and its illumination that welcomed me in the dead of night, I see just one single streetlight that offers great clarity. And this reminds me of one of those few funny stories I can recall, like the one where a man is at the foot of a lamppost searching for his keys. A passerby stops to ask if he is sure he lost them there. "No," he replies, "but I'll only be able to find them here."

To rediscover the path to the workshop, I would start from this point, sliding into the enchantment of the alleyways, orienting myself with the inspiration of the moment, breathing in the ancient air that arises from one of these corridors, as though a hand is reaching out, in a bookstore, from the binding of an old volume.

Back then, I lived near the Hôtel de Ville and it was the inevitable path and point of departure for a new adventure. What a great adventure it was. During the week, I would add some pages to my novel, *Don Juan*, and tremble with the anticipation of reading them to Marianne. These moments would take on great importance for her, too. She would listen to me with rapt attention; I would even say in a state of intense concentration. A deep trust grew between us. We spoke heart to heart.

This was during the late 1970s and the early 1980s. Before beginning *Don Juan*, I read her some texts that pleased her. One day, in the middle of a reading, she exclaimed, throwing her arms into the air, "My life will have been complete. I'll even have witnessed the birth of a great writer!"

Of course, I say this with the utmost humility; I even dare say it with humor, which, for Marianne, was the mark of its seriousness. Of course, she thought so, but she was especially amenable to the pleasure in sharing a moment of calm, of true stillness, imagining together a landscape where anything could suddenly appear or conjure itself, as in the image of a vast plain from one of Garcia Lorca's poems, which echoes with horse hooves like the beating of a drum.

Standing before her painting, *Don Juan*, which she painted during that time, you would understand. It is quite evocative of the metaphysical solitude in which Marianne evolved, populated with rugged cliffs, which one had to scale alongside her to keep up.

For me, she is best described by the image of an alchemist.

The image that I'm portraying does not attempt to be flattering, but fair. And I believe that I'm arriving at the truth. In any case, there is another side to the coin, which back then was not apparent to me, or that I chose to leave in the shadows.

The attraction of Marianne often made us lose our sense of reality. In the athanor[1] of her workshop, everything was vividly colored, bathed in a magic glow, under the smoky cloud of our cigarettes.

I never became a great writer, except according to a few dear friends, who are not only dear because they think this. No publisher wanted my *Don Juan.* Marianne herself, after I had finished it, expressed reservations when I'd talk about its publication. She postponed week after week to give it to friends to read, as she had promised me. When, one day, they did return their verdict, it was not positive. Marianne had suddenly changed her mind. She talked about corrections without adding precision. It would be better for me, she added, to write something entirely different.

If I linger over this episode, it's because it's a clear example that our elation can impair us at certain times, only to be brought back down, like a soufflé deflating to the airlessness of reality. Freud spoke of a death instinct. Regarding this instinct, he added, "Within the libido ('the energetic manifestation of

---

1 An athanor is a self-feeding digesting furnace that maintains a uniform and durable heat and was used by alchemists, according to *Merriam-Webster.*

Eros'), we can but discern its presence as a residue, glimpsed beneath erotic manifestations, *which eludes us as soon as its blending with them no longer betrays it.*"[2]

In the same sense, and using the same exact words, one could speak about Marianne, the instinct for defeat, a will to fail.

An instinct and a desire, very much hidden beneath erotic manifestations. "We are in love, are we not, us two," she would say to me often. Without a doubt, I couldn't help but admit it, but what was unspoken was that this love was demanding, exclusive, excessive. In a word: surrealist.

Her recompense was that I belonged to her, and with my *Don Juan*, she kept me waiting a long while, one might say, in Kantian terms, "without visibility of an end,"[3] a state Marianne referred to as "the frustration of desire." Within this anticipation, she held me captive.

It was a delightful prison, I must admit. We were never lovers, it should be said. With incredible patience, she instilled

---

2 Emphasis is the author's own.

3 In Kant's writing on eschatology, "The End of All Things" (1794), the concept of the end is a construct of reason, it is unknowable through human experience. "Here we are . . . playing with ideas created by reason itself . . . whose objects lie wholly beyond our vision." Immanuel Kant, "The End of All Things [*Das Ende aller Dinge*] (1794)" in *Religion and Rational Theology*, trans. Allen W. Wood and George di Giovanni, 217–232, *The Cambridge Edition of the Works of Immanuel Kant* (Cambridge: Cambridge University Press, 1996).

a will to fail in me, finally leading me to explode in an outburst when faced with her request that I revise *Don Juan* or "leave it on the shelf."

There was undoubtedly a good reason for revision, one which I came to understand when Marianne recounted a humiliation she had suffered in a gallery, where she had come to propose a book written by her husband, Radovan Ivsic. It was a very beautiful draft, enriched with a lithograph by Jean Miró, which the gallerist promptly tore out of the binding before throwing the rest of the work in the trash bin.

After my outburst, Marianne had a heart attack. To her, it was clear that I had wanted to kill her. It felt like the ceiling, she told me, had caved in on her head, a ceiling that she had significantly weakened by detaching a wooden pillar from the plaster, as well as the joists. Additionally, it was not only the ceiling of her studio that had collapsed but every floor in the house.

Worry began to consume me. Should I blame her? The thought never crossed my mind. These were the rules of the game. It was my fault for not having understood them.

We had really laughed together; we had truly marveled in one another.

Marianne stayed very reticent about her experience fighting against fascism with the Yugoslav Partisans. However, she confided in me two memories that remained vivid for her.

The first was of an injured soldier who asked her for food when his comrades had nothing more to offer him. Marianne and some others approached a farm to ask for an egg. The farmers refused. "An egg, can you believe it? And they had no desire to trade!" Her face burned with anger.

The second was one of a young fighter who had become close with Marianne and was placed under her protection. One day, when he had to leave for military observation, he asked Marianne to take his coat, which, he said, was bulletproof. Marianne did what she could to put him off the idea, but at the young man's insistence, she finally conceded. Moved by this memory, Marianne left a heavy pause, then added very quickly, "He was killed that day."

Marianne was buried at Montparnasse Cemetery. On her tombstone, I suggested engraving only the words of her motto: "*Ama et fac quod vis.*" Love and do what you want.

This happened without me having to ask twice. I am grateful to the friends who made the funeral arrangements.

That was more than twenty years ago. *Twenty Years After* is the title Alexandre Dumas gave the sequel to his *Three Musketeers*. Marianne liked to tell us there had once been a blacksmith living in her courtyard, and D'Artagnan, the fourth of the three musketeers, used to bring him his horse. How did she know this? The way she spoke about it while looking at the courtyard, one could have believed that the blacksmith had only ceased working there a few weeks before.

I spoke to her one day about this sequel that Alexandre Dumas had given to his most famous work. I promised to bring her a copy. It was Christmas. After dining at my parents' place, I set off, the book in my arms. It was already well past midnight, and I had a long journey ahead. I had to traverse almost all of Paris on foot, but the night was so beautiful. Snow had fallen. In front of the Louvre, I slipped on the pathway but got straight back up unharmed. I had narrowly avoided a fracture.

As it was so late when I entered Marianne's courtyard, we had agreed that I would not knock on the door. I approached the window. One of the tiny windowpanes was open.

I slipped the book in at the very moment that Marianne held out her hand.

Marianne Ivsic
Don Juan, 1981
Oil on canvas
34 × 27 cm

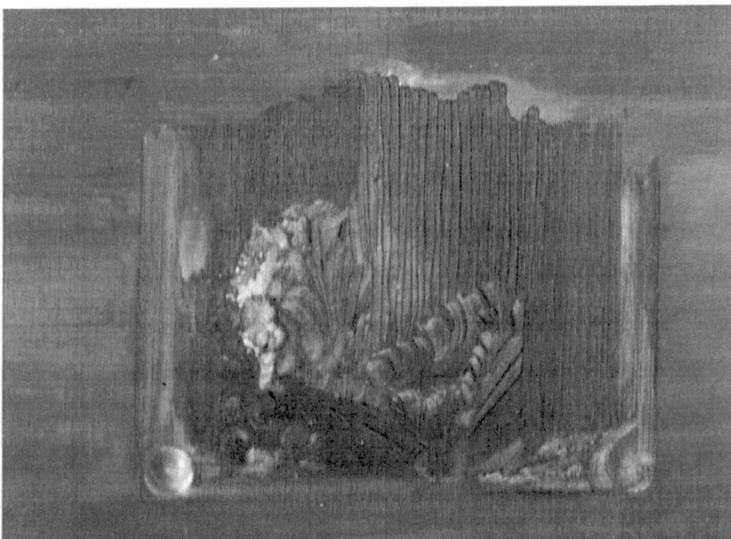

Marianne had her atelier in the small lodging to the right.

You can see the dark outline of the window where I slipped the book to her late one Christmas night.

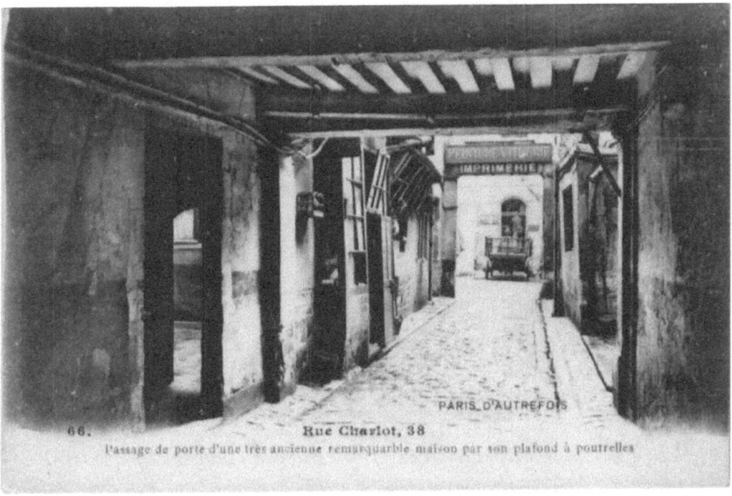

66. **Rue Charlot, 38**

Passage de porte d'une très ancienne remarquable maison par son plafond à poutrelles

When her landlord evicted her from the rue Galande apartment, Marianne left with the promise of finding this dwelling in the Temple District. Back then, real estate investors hadn't yet converted all the artist studios into "lofts."

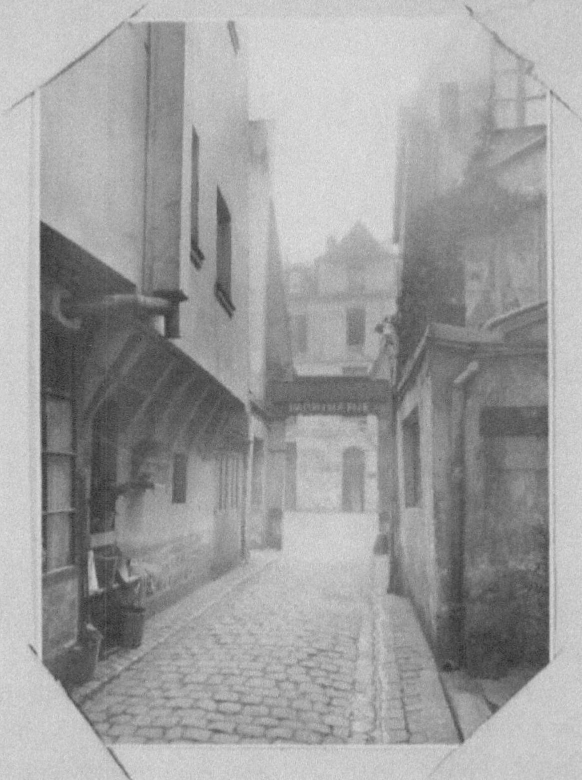

38 rue Charlot

When Marianne lived in the square, a door
had been carved into the wall, where it descended to the gutter.
She presided over the entrance to her atelier.
On this door, I discovered her name written in chalk.

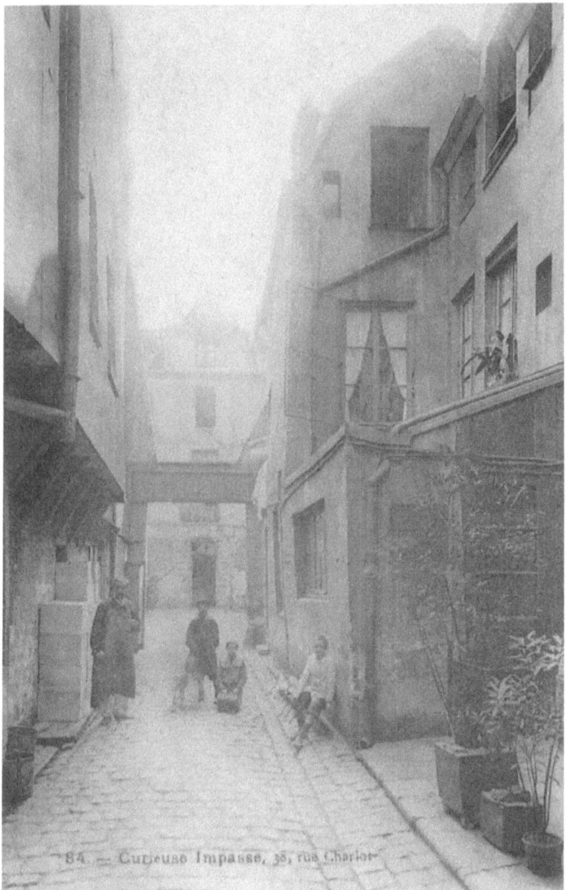
84. — Curieuse Impasse, 38, rue Charlot
Vieux Paris B. C. (déposé)

MUSKETEER

He was a long-time friend, but we were hardly close. We first met in the mid-1960s. René Viénet was a member of the prestigious Situationist International. This qualifier would have made him smile. But my comrades and I, we were so amazed by the Situationists back then.

I have already written about that first meeting, one winter evening, in a café on the Place de la République. Upon entering, it was actually his friend Donald Nicholson-Smith who caught my eye, with his dignified beard—like Mikhail Bakunin. René was wearing a blue jacket, which I thought was very lightweight, considering the season. I had also noticed two young women of distinct beauty who accompanied them. The room was empty apart from us.

We were four or five members from various anarchist groups, and the Situationists were doing us the honor of meeting with us. A highly irregular favor on their part. They had maintained an almost distant air, or, at least, that's what I believed then. Later, I understood I'd been mistaken. They were not aiming to create distance; I think they were even saddened by it. But their revolutionary critique left them isolated, bereft of interlocutors who could satisfy their requirements.

While Donald grew an anarchist's beard, René contented himself with a thin blonde moustache. His blue jacket could have been a sailor's or a longshoreman's peacoat. I came to understand this better when I learned that his father was a docker. When he stood up to reveal his tall figure, he was something of a giant. But the best image I can use to describe him is one of a musketeer, grander than D'Artagnan, with his mid-length hair, his blue eyes, and his dignified moustache.

Today, I know his age, and I can tell you that he was twenty-two, while I was barely seventeen. And if today I know this, his age, it's because we saw each other fifty years later, and he is now seventy-eight. Just a few weeks ago, I saw him again: a miracle, or perhaps just coincidence, which amounts to the same thing.

I was writing several lines in my *Knights* wherein I spoke about him. He had learned about this text and expressed a desire to meet with me. So, we began exchanging our first messages. As they often do, the events had silently woven together to reunite the players from across the years.

During the pandemic, René arranged to meet me in a beloved book shop, which served as his lair, and where, he assured me they would serve us coffee. My feeling about meeting him again was much like the first time. Except that, at that time, I had only opened my mouth to greet him. I had before me one of those remarkable men who one never forgets having had the good fortune of meeting. Our handshake that day held a certain weight. It recalled those fragmented memories of poetry and history; all things blended together. It confirmed the image I held of him, of a Musketeer. His features bore a notable distinction.

My memories had touched him. He was having a hard time, recollecting now, and I had helped him recall them. I had an even stronger impulse to guide him; when he had to leave to run an errand, I proposed that I accompany him. His powerful stature now had something of a frailty to it. It seemed to me that he would find the journey easier with me.

Those paces down the street, in the busy throng, remain special to me. It was an exquisite moment which, to this day, leaves me in total awe. We were two survivors of a sunken galleon; we walked in a cloud of gold dust, glimmering in silence, almost shoulder to shoulder as the path narrowed. Like those times when we sat in a café, around a table.

THE DAY IS A BRIDGE, THE NIGHT IS A DOOR

We knew the meeting had taken place, but our doubts remained until Alice sent around four photos—we'd only known about one. Four pieces of proof of her stay in Vosges in August 1968, with Marianne, Guy, and an unidentified young man who was a friend of Pierre Lepetit.

Until then, we doubted that such a meeting had indeed occurred. We learned that there was a photo showing Marianne, Alice, and Guy together.

This photo had been lost by the very person who assured us of its existence. It was Alice Becker-Ho who rediscovered other photos taken back then in her personal archives. It was not what we were searching for, but Alice's photos exceeded our expectations. And we had not expected to receive so many of them.

We were on a fragile, unstable bridge. Then, the castle door, behind the bridge, was opened. It was more than just evidence: it was a confession; because a confession is willing to tell. It took us in and redeemed us by dissipating our doubts. We had crossed the threshold as if pushed by the same gust of wind that carried our hesitations, questions, and uncertainties. In our quest, we had been granted access to the Castle Perilous.[1]

Four black-and-white photographs show murky undergrowth and a house lost in the heart of the forest, where nothing leads except the compelling desire to be close to these characters of rare individual destinies. Even more, because they were close to one another.

Suddenly, the atmosphere between us was different. The raised drawbridge was transformed into a portal, which retained us with an enchantment, just like when Vivian imprisoned Merlin, with a spell, in a glass tower.

It was indeed enchanting to find the house and its occupants in the forest. The path that led there could only appear as a single track by the grace of a sudden light falling from the sky and a gust of wind that brushed the ferns aside.

It was a house of dark wood, as if singed by a great fire that had blackened the boards. A few steps in front of the entrance, Guy is just inside the door, Marianne is standing, next to an anonymous young man. She posed with a hand

---

1 A reference to one of many castles in the *Tales of the Knights of the Holy Grail.* In Arthurian legend, the Castle Perilous first appears in *Le Morte D'Arthur* by Sir Thomas Malory (1469). It is where Sir Gareth faces challenges of his determination and bravery, to rescue the captive Lady Lyonesse. Thomas Malory, "How Sir Gareth Came to the Presence of His Lady," in *Le Morte D'Arthur, Vol. I* (Book VII, Chapter XXI), Project Gutenberg, https://www.gutenberg.org/files/1251/1251-h/1251-h.htm.

on his shoulder as if she were dubbing a knight. Alice, of course, took the picture.

Their immobility is troubling but also touching. Their expressions look grave, though nothing implies this; everything demands it because, after fifty years, someone has come to look at them. Though not quite believing it at first; later we could only marvel at it.

The meeting of the three friends who are searching them had been set long ago. They have no aim other than to confound us and surprise us, we who had our doubts.

Their expressions seem to say, "You have taken the time. Finally, you have arrived."

Guy Debord (in window),
Marianne Ivsic,
and Roger Legarec, a friend of Pierre Lepetit (seated).
Lepetit was the owner of the house in Vosges. At the time, he shared Marianne's life.
Vosges, August 1968.

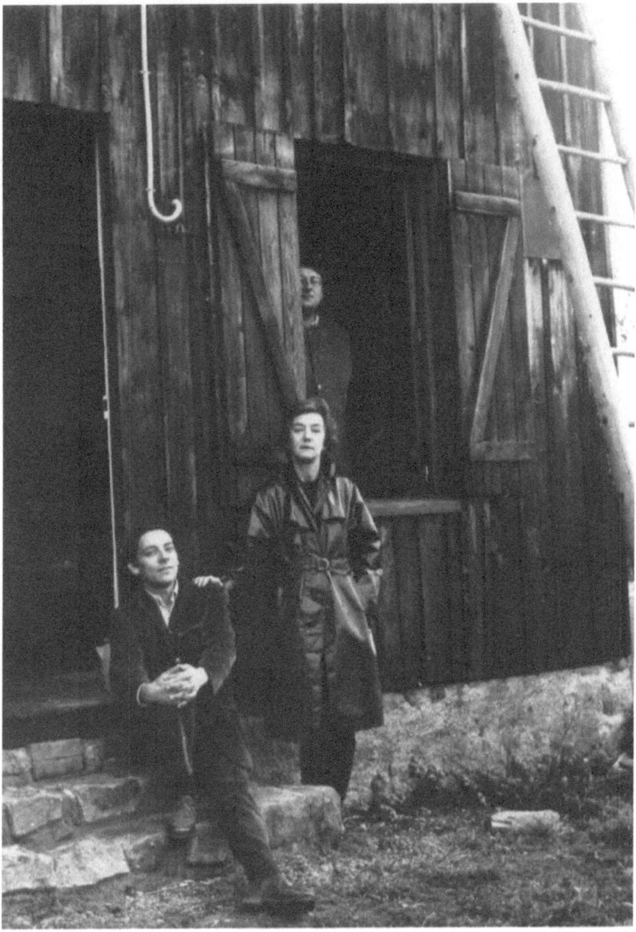

Marianne Ivsic and Alice Becker-Ho, aka Alice Debord.
Vosges, August 1968.

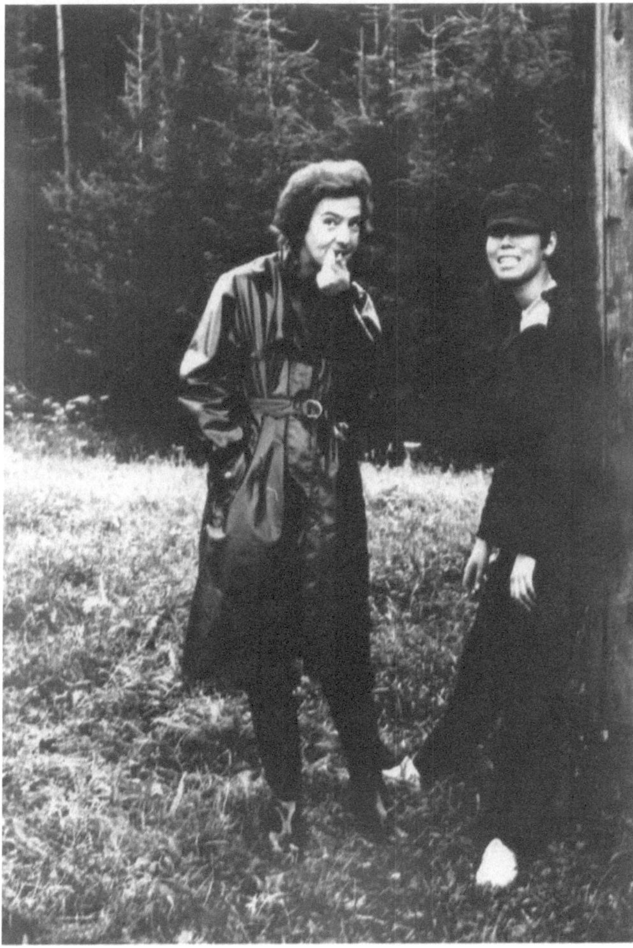

Our time hasn't passed us by.
We only moved beyond it.

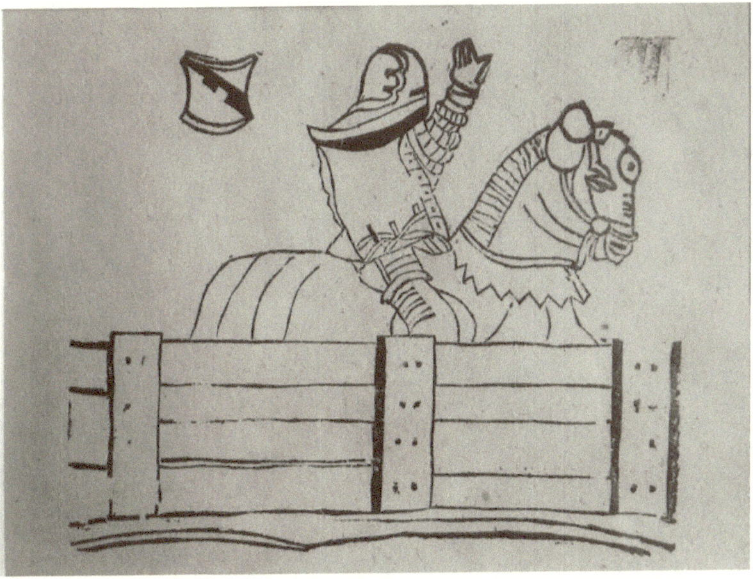

ABOUT THE AUTHOR

Alain Segura was born in 1949, in Bellac, a town near Limoges, France, where his father, active as an anarchist militant in Spain, settled after the Civil War of 1936–1939. In his teens, he was a member of several small anarchist groups, including the Anarchist International.

ABOUT THE TRANSLATORS

Anna O'Meara is a Ph.D. Candidate in Art History & Visual Studies at the University of Victoria. Her dissertation research investigates how the Situationist concept of Spectacle relates to World. Anna is coeditor of *On the Poverty of Student Life: Considered in Its Economic, Political, Psychological, Sexual, and Particularly Intellectual Aspects, and a Modest Proposal for Its Remedy* (Common Notions, 2022). Her translations have been published by Three Rooms Press, Verso, and Annex Press, among others.

Sarah Lynne Roberts is a PhD student in Art History Visual Studies at the University of Victoria. She studies surrealist intersections with Latin American film from a feminist perspective. She holds an MA in Art History Visual Studies from the University of Victoria and a BA in Art History and Visual Culture with proficiency in French from the University of Exeter. Born in Watford, England, she lives in Victoria, BC, on the unceded territories of the Lekwungen peoples.

ABOUT COMMON NOTIONS

Common Notions is a publishing house and programming platform that fosters new formulations of living autonomy. We aim to circulate timely reflections, clear critiques, and inspiring strategies that amplify movements for social justice.

Our publications trace a constellation of critical and visionary meditations on the organization of freedom. By any media necessary, we seek to nourish the imagination and generalize common notions about the creation of other worlds beyond state and capital. Inspired by various traditions of autonomism and liberation—in the US and internationally, historical and emerging from contemporary movements—our publications provide resources for a collective reading of struggles past, present, and to come.

Common Notions regularly collaborates with political collectives, militant authors, radical presses, and maverick designers around the world. Our political and aesthetic pursuits are dreamed and realized with Antumbra Designs.

www.commonnotions.org
info@commonnotions.org

COMMON NOTIONS

BECOME A COMMON NOTIONS MONTHLY SUSTAINER

These are decisive times ripe with challenges and possibility, heartache, and beautiful inspiration. More than ever, we need timely reflections, clear critiques, and inspiring strategies that can help movements for social justice grow and transform society.

Help us amplify those words, deeds, and dreams that our liberation movements, and our worlds, so urgently need.

Movements are sustained by people like you, whose fugitive words, deeds, and dreams bend against the world of domination and exploitation.

For collective imagination, dedicated practices of love and study, and organized acts of freedom.
By any media necessary.
With your love and support.
Monthly sustainers start at $15 and receive each new book in our publishing program.

commonnotions.org/sustain

MORE FROM COMMON NOTIONS

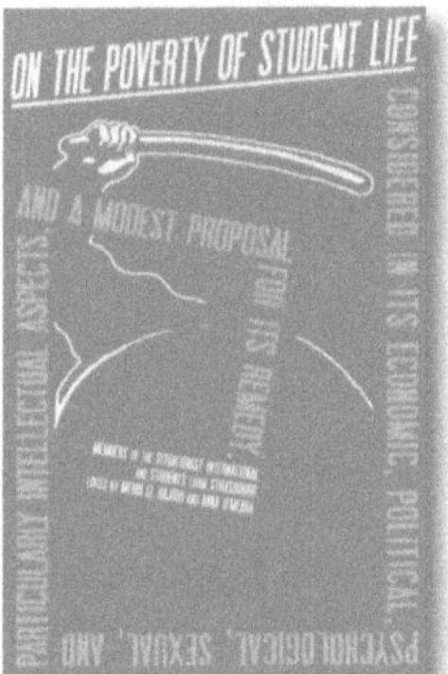

On the Poverty of Student Life

Considered in Its Economic, Political, Psychological, Sexual, and Particularly Intellectual Aspects, and a Modest Proposal for Its Remedy

Members of The Situationist International & Students From Strasbourg, Edited by Mehdi El Hajoui and Anna O'Meara

978-1-942173-57-1
Paperback | 376 pages | 6 x 9 in | $24
Education | Anticapitalism | Situationist

The manifesto that launched the Situationist International (SI) into the public eye and sparked an uprising is back—with the story of its creation and the histories of its publication told.

Featuring the original English adaptation by former SI member and celebrated translator Donald Nicholson-Smith, an interview with primary author Mustapha Khayati where he traces his map from colonial Algeria to imperial France, and essays about the political relevance of the manifesto—an edition like this has never before existed. With beautiful photographs of nearly one hundred different editions this book provides a cartography of an uprising.

MORE FROM COMMON NOTIONS

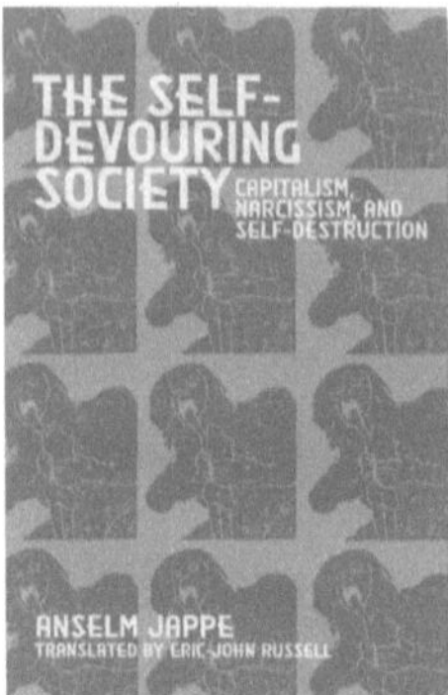

The Self-Devouring Society

Capitalism, Narcissism, and Self-Destruction

Anselm Jappe, Translated by Eric-John Russell

978-1-942173-79-3
Paperback | 256 pages | 5.5 x 8.5 in | $24
Critical Theory | Capitalism | Psychology

Renowned theorist Anselm Jappe explains how contemporary capitalism has turned everyone into a narcissist.

In a work that unites the critique of political economy and the psychoanalytic tradition, Jappe explores the dynamics of contemporary capitalism and explains how internalizing them creates a specific kind of person—a narcissist, someone who can only interact with the world by consuming it and who cannot conceive of limits to this consumption. In conversation with Marx as well as Freud, Erich Fromm, Herbert Marcuse, and Christopher Lasch, Jappe probes the ways in which the churning of the capitalist machine, ceaseless and yet devoid of real purpose, creates an endless hunger that increasingly ends in spectacular violence.

MORE FROM COMMON NOTIONS

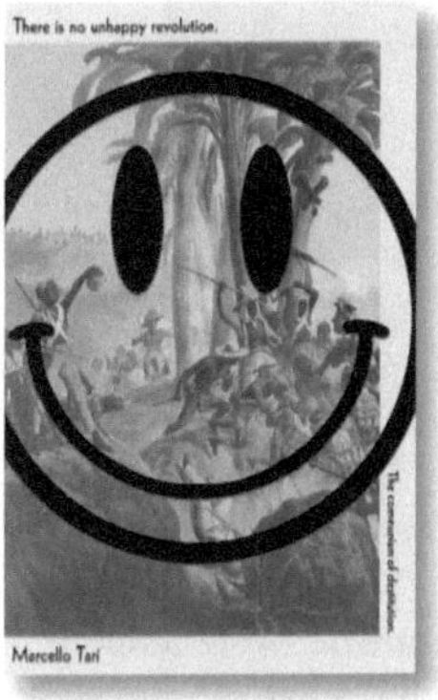

There Is No Unhappy Revolution

The Communism of Destitution

Marcello Tarì, Translated by Richard Braude

978-1-942173-16-8
Paperback | 244 pages | 5.5 x 8.5 in | $18
Politics | Philosophy | Communism

In a era of ongoing political, economic, and climate crisis, Marcello Tarì reclaims the revolutionary task of making life worth living :)

Can we afford our collective unhappiness any longer? *There Is No Unhappy Revolution* gives expression to the age of revolution unfolding before us.

Offering both a militant philosophy and a philosophy of militancy, he deftly confronts the different contemporary movements from the Argentinean insurrection of 2001 to Occupy Wall Street, the Spanish Indignados, the French movement against the labor law, and the Arab spring, resurrecting and renewing a destituent lineage of revolutionary thought, from Walter Benjamin to Giorgio Agamben, that promises to make life livable.

MORE FROM COMMON NOTIONS

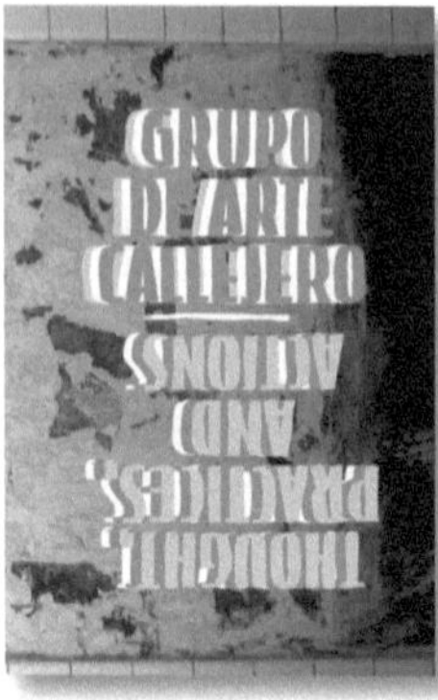

Grupo de Arte Callejero

Thought, Practices, and Actions

Grupo de Arte Callejero, Translated by the Mareada Rosa Translation Collective

978-1-942173-10-6
Paperback | 352 pages | 6 x 9 in | $22
Art | Latin America | Social Theory

From a legendary feminist art collective in Argentina, an indispensible reflection on what was done and what remains to be done in the social fields of art and revolution.

Grupo de Arte Callejero: Thought, Practices, and Actions tells the profound story of social militancy and art in Argentina over the last two decades and propels it forward. For Grupo de Arte Callejero [Group of Street Artists], militancy and art blur together in the anonymous, collective, everyday spaces and rhythms of life. Thought, Practices, and Actions offers an indispensable reflection on what was done and what remains to be done in the social fields of art and revolution.

www.ingramcontent.com/pod-product-compliance
Lightning Source LLC
La Vergne TN
LVHW100347150926
847902LV00024B/180